FRAME
THE RED PILL
WORKBOOK

DAVID L. BAUER

ISBN: 978-1-946629-90-6

Morpheus to Neo: *(The Matrix)* This is your last chance. After this, there is no turning back. You take the blue pill, the story ends. You wake up in your bed and believe whatever you want to. You take the red pill, you stay in Wonderland, and I show you how deep the rabbit hole goes. Remember, all I'm offering is the truth. Nothing more.

Neo: What truth?

Morpheus: That you are a slave, Neo. Like everyone else you were born into bondage. Into a prison that you cannot taste or see or touch. A prison for your mind.

Purpose

What truth? What is truth?

The purpose of this book is to provide a method for men to discover their own truth, the truth of who they authentically are. Every man has the ability, and indeed the right and responsibility, to decide for themselves their own truth of who they are. We, as men, decide our boundaries and convictions. We decide what we will and will not stand for. We decide who we are and are not.

In doing so, we all must be willing to accept the truth. We must be willing to look at ourselves objectively. We must be willing to accept reality as it currently exists.

In doing so, we must be open and willing to change for the better.

In doing so, we must become totally self-responsible and internally motivated. We are responsible to get our own needs met. We are responsible for everything that shows up in our lives, the good, the bad, the ugly, and the beautiful. We cannot allow ourselves to be influenced by outside forces or other people's demands and expectations.

In doing so, we must commit to setting our boundaries and pushing back without emotion when they are violated. This is especially true when being tested. We must push back <u>every</u> time we are tested. If we let it slide, the next test becomes that much more challenging.

Two Worlds

Everyone grows up in a reality of two worlds.

The first is the world we can see, the external world, where the laws of physics and nature always apply. It is a world of logic, cause and effect, and reason. It is the world described by Newton's Laws. We grow up depending on its validity and consistency. For boys, it is the world that is exclusively emphasized.

The second is the internal, unseen but important world of thoughts, emotions, psyche, and soul. For boys, this is the part of them that is usually neglected, even suppressed, or repressed. Boys learn at a very early age that crying is not okay, and by extension, your feelings are not okay. Boys are taught to ignore their feelings even when it hurts; that equals toughness. Showing emotions is considered weakness. Our inner life is ignored first by parents and caregivers, then by ourselves. Boys socialized in this way continue to ignore their feelings through school, including college, and into their marriage, as many of us have. Then later, our inner life is disregarded by others, including our life partners.

Often, the outcomes in those first relationships are not happy or successful.

What I Believe

What I believe is very simple. I believe our highest purpose is to grow our inner life – ourselves. For myself, personal growth is my highest priority, and it's a trait I admire in others. If I am working on myself, my life smooths out, my relationships work effortlessly. My effort is placed on working on myself, my internal strength, courage, knowledge, and self-awareness – my inner life.

It is a lifelong process.

"The better ambitions have to do with the development of character and ability, as opposed to status and power. Status you can lose. Character and ability, you carry with you wherever you go, and it allows you to prevail against adversity."

—Jordan B. Peterson, Ph.D.

We, as men, must do our inner work. It is not enough to do our outside work. Yes, one can do well in school and sports, do a good job, be a good person, earn money, have material things, and be outwardly successful. That is not enough. We must do our inner work to move beyond external success. We all must work on our inner life, which is far more important than the external. If we do not, women will continue to move ahead of us in personal growth and development.

Life Is Difficult

You think your life is great, perfect, and then someone throws a hanging curve directly at your head.

My wife of 24 years had returned from a trip to New Zealand and Australia with one of her girlfriends. While she was happy to be back after a long trip, I sensed something was off. Something wasn't right with her, or between us.

This was the first time we had to sit down and really talk since her return. This is the conversation:

J: We've been needing to talk. I have something I need to talk about – something important.

D: Sounds serious.

J: It is. This is hard for me to talk about. It was hard to admit to myself, much less talk about with you.

D: Oh. Okay, I am listening.

J: Well, she and I spent most of our time in New Zealand with her single friends. I became aware that I sort of liked the freedom they—the single ones—had. I became aware that I was envious of the freedom they had to be with anyone they wanted.

D: Sounds like I should have gone with you.

J: Yes, you should have, but you didn't, did you?

D: No, I didn't.

J: So, as I was saying, I was envious of their single lifestyle and had the thought that maybe I would like to be single again.

D: You can't be serious. *(Actually, she could be. I was often confused about where I stood with her, despite the fact we had been married for nearly 24 years.)*

J: I am not saying I want to split up, but I am not happy. I am really not happy with the way things are between us right now.

D: I think I hear you, but I don't really understand … unhappy how? *(I knew that whether she loved me or not was dependent on how she felt in any given moment, and that could, and often did, change moment to moment. I could sense this was something deeper.)*

J: Well, for one thing, it seems like you are zoned out all the time. You are not present with me or the kids or the grandkids. You are on your phone or your computer or watching football or otherwise zoned out.

D: Well, okay, I guess I must admit that might be true some of the time. *(I could feel myself zoning out as she was talking.)*

J: The way I see it, it is most of the time. But the real problem is that you don't ever push back when I challenge you. You never disagree with me. Whatever I say or do, you just go along with.

D: Well, okay, I do think that I am easy to get along with. Are you saying that is a problem for you now?

J: Yeah, the problem is you are too easy to get along with, and you are too nice. It's kind of sickening.

D: Wow, I had no idea!

J: I have thought about it a lot, and I am sure that is the problem, for me anyway.

D: Well, I always thought I was the type of guy you wanted.

J: You were. That's true. You were. And then I found out that wasn't attractive to me. I thought I wanted someone like my daddy, and when I got him, it was a big turn-off. I found out that's not what I wanted. So, I'm sorry.

D: What am I supposed to say to that?

J: I don't know, but honestly, that's where I'm at. I just don't know what I am going to do.

D: What does that mean?

J: You know I am starting my sabbatical this month.

D: I know you mentioned it.

J: I am going to take the next six months off, and during that time, I am going to make some decisions. One will be about us. So, how things go during the next six months will determine what I decide about us.

D: Sounds like how I perform as a husband is going to be tested for the next six months!

J: No, it's more about our relationship and how we interact in our relationship that will help me make up my mind.

D: What are you expecting from me?

J: I don't know, but I am sure you will figure it out. I will let you know what I decide in June.

D: Oh – okay.

Shock and Denial

Shock and denial? For sure! I initially thought to myself, "This can't be happening to me. What the hell is going on with her?" We had been happily married for nearly 24 years, or so I thought. She had in fact expressed her love and devotion many times over those many years. Now she was saying she did not or wasn't sure whether or not she loved me. Talk about a cheap trick! I was angry as all hell.

In the days that followed, I observed her going about her life, and it appeared that everything was fine. For her, everything seemed normal. For me, however, it was turmoil. It was self-doubt. It was self-criticism. My self-talk was anything but positive.

Some days I avoided thinking about things and zoned out, my usual way of coping. Other days, I was focused on something else, the stock market, a distraction. I questioned everything I did, especially if it involved interacting with her.

It became apparent that sex was less important to her and that she was not as physically attracted to me as she once had been. That was the point of crisis that shifted me into thinking that I was not going to be able to change her. If I were going to attract her again, I would need to change myself. Change myself how?

I thought, "She has been working on turning me into a blue-pill beta wimp like her father, and it hasn't worked out so well for either one of us. Now what?"

I may have been angry with her, but I was even more upset with myself for not seeing it as it was happening. I was pissed at myself for letting it happen!

Blue-Pill Beta Wimp

What was my truth?

Upon making a searching and fearless self-inventory, I concluded that I had taken the blue pill without realizing it. I had no frame!

I was not showing up in the relationship. I was not present in the marriage. I was on my phone; I was too easy to get along with; I was too nice; I was on my computer. During the week, I was watching stocks and, on the weekend, I was watching football. Not to mention the glass or two of wine in the evenings.

As a result of not being present, I never pushed back. So, from her point of view, it was like not being in a relationship at all. There was never anyone for her to push against nor to push back against her.

I was truly screwed up! The question really should be: What are all the ways my life was adversely impacted? When I really stepped back and took a good hard look at it, this presented many different problems, all of which could be traced back to my lack of frame. Here is the list:

- I was passive. As a result, I did not push back when she challenged me. I was too easy to get along with, and too nice.

- I was externally referenced, influenced too much by the perceived expectations of others, especially her, but also others. This in turn cast me into the victim role in many interactions, without me being totally conscious of it.

- I was not self-responsible. It had never occurred to me that I needed to be responsible for myself and everything that showed up in my life.

- I was lacking self-awareness most of the time and was not present-oriented. I was not particularly aware of my thoughts and feelings, nor what they might be telling me about a current situation, often thinking about the future or past instead of staying in the present.

- Often, I had no opinion. I wouldn't take a position on anything for fear of displeasing someone. This showed up in ridiculous ways; for example, on a road trip, if someone asked, "Do you want to stop at the next convenience store?" Instead of yes or no, I would say, "I'm good either way."

So, after going over this list, I had to admit it was at least partially true. I realized that I was responsible for my behavior, and I could change my behavior. Admitting that, I could then begin to search for answers or solutions. What needed to change? How should I change?

I had already been doing research; however, my motivation increased dramatically now that the research applied to me. Positive, self-directed, sustainable change is what I was seeking.

The problems, it seems, began years before, seeded in my childhood and early life.

Manners Can Be Fun

I was four years old. We had a console RCA record player in the family room. I was playing a record titled *Manners Can Be Fun* over and over. On this day, I was playing nearby while listening to the recording. Of course, like any kid, I wasn't paying attention and bumped into the record player, sending the needle skipping loudly across the record. *Skreeeeeeeeeeeecchh!*

My mother came unglued, took me by the arm, and dragged me into the kitchen where she took a yardstick and proceeded to beat me repeatedly on the bottom. She hit me so hard and so many times that the yardstick broke into three pieces. I don't remember the pain, but I do remember the broken pieces of yardstick.

These types of beatings continued for the next four years, until we moved to a new house and I entered third grade.

Wash Your Mouth

I was five years old, outside riding my bicycle. It was a beautiful Saturday morning. The air smelled fresh and clean. I had been doing a good job of staying within my boundaries: 10th Street to the north, 11th Street south, Duluth Ave east, and Summit, where we lived, to the west. A one-block area, clear and simple boundaries for a five-year-old.

I had not been riding that new bike long, having just learned. I had also been learning other new things. My friend Rich, who lived at the other end of the block, was three years older, and much wiser. He knew a lot more. What was Rich teaching me? Within the last day or so, I had learned "shit." Of course, Rich hadn't told me what it meant, and he also left out the fact that you couldn't say it around adults. Naturally, I was eager to try out my new vocabulary.

I was riding south on the sidewalk from Rich's. As I approached my house, I became vaguely aware that both my parents were on the front porch working or cleaning something. Beyond them, I saw my friend Jimmy riding his bike toward me from the other direction. As I rode closer, I yelled at the top of my lungs, "Hey, Jimmy, you shit!"

Suddenly, as if struck by lightning, I found himself in the kitchen, mom and dad on either side, yelling at me. Then my mouth was pried open and a bar of Ivory soap jammed into it. I just stood there choking on it, tearing up, and listening to mom say, "I'm going to leave this in your mouth long enough for you to think about how you talk."

I remember the soap wrapper, "Ivory Soap, 99 and 44/100 percent pure."

My external reference was firmly locked in place for the next 37 years.

Plan of Attack

My plan of attack—how to strengthen my internal character and value—had two aspects to it.

The first aspect, the objective, was to shift permanently to internal reference (vs. external).

I had become aware of my tendency to be almost totally externally referenced earlier in life. In fact, I had done a lot of work toward better internal reference in therapy years ago. Apparently, I had slipped back into the external mode of living and being without realizing what had happened to me.

The second aspect, the how, was to build and strengthen my frame.

I had read about the concept of physical frame while researching masculinity. I had also seen the concept applied to other aspects of a person's life. The concept of frame as I envision it would be like a picture frame with four corners: physical, mental, emotional, and spiritual. The picture within the frame is the person's life, work, and relationships. Each of the four corners of the frame would need to be anchored by boundaries, values, and convictions. I would need to decide what those were, write them down, remember them, and most importantly, live them by pushing back when tested.

My frame supports my mission in life, which is to coach young men of all ages on their relationships, as well as supporting my interactions in my significant relationships: my wife, children, and grandchildren.

To live my frame, I would need to be aware when it was being tested, bent, or violated. This was most important and most challenging when relating in my most important relationship – my marriage.

I would require myself to speak up when I perceived my frame was being tested. Speaking up when being tested is not optional; it is mandatory. Let me say that again. You must say something every time you are tested. If you don't speak up, things will only get worse.

"Regardless of how many years you have been on the wrong path,
you can stop and turn to the right path."

—Author unknown

First Step – Complete the following exercises.

EXERCISES

Prerequisite Needs

Everyone requires their most basic physical human needs be met.

Physical needs:

1. Air

2. Water

3. Food

4. Shelter

5. Sleep

Beyond physical needs, we have other more complex needs we seek to fulfill. Here are some examples of psychological needs:

1. Significance

2. To love and be loved

3. Contribution

4. Certainty

5. Variety

6. Growth

For a more complete picture relating to yourself, do the needs exercise beginning on the next page.

Meeting Your Own Needs

People can usually remember a time in early life when they became less concerned about their own needs and became more concerned about the needs of others or about pressure from the outside world to conform. That is called external reference or locus of control.

Now, it is time to identify and name your unmet needs. A *need* is something you must have in order for you to be authentically who you are. This is what YOU need, not what <u>others</u> think you need or what you think you <u>should</u> need.

Refer to the following *Needs List*. Read through this list, notice any emotional reaction you have to specific words, and circle them. Prioritize, until you can list your top three unmet needs.

Needs List			
Respect	Affection	To Love	To Be Correct
Honesty	Achievement	To Be Valued	To Be Heard/Listened to
Recognition	Fairness	To Be Loved	Autonomy, More Freedom
Influence	Security	To Be Creative	Balance and Unity
Stimulation	Fun	To Feel Special	Calmness/Peace
Trust	Appreciation	To Give	To Do the Right Thing
Leadership	Praise	To Be Included	To Be Important
Fulfillment	Order	To Be Needed	To Be Wanted
Acceptance	Encouragement	Attention/Notice	To Be Competent
To Be Wanted	To Be Safe	To Self-express	To Experience Adventure
Friendship	Acknowledgment	To Be Cared for	To Be Honored

List your top three needs:

1. ....

2. ....

3. ....

There are three primary ways to get a need met:

- **Fulfill the need yourself by developing new personal habits.**

- **Enforce or set a boundary.** (Start or practice saying "No" occasionally)

- **Eliminate something you are tolerating.**

All three ways to get a need met are your responsibility and are to be accomplished by you.

Remember: Spiritual maturity is when you take **100%** of the responsibility for whatever shows up in your life. This means learning to meet your own needs *from the inside out*.

Tolerations Exercise

I think of tolerations as the opposite of needs. Tolerations are things you do not want or need in your life. Eliminating something you are tolerating is always an indication something better is on the way. Something must be deleted if we are to get the good we desire in our lives.

Ask yourself: *"**What am I willing to give up in order to get what I really want?**"*

In the chart below, make a list of all the things you have been tolerating or putting up with in your outside life, where your boundaries have been crossed. Next to each item, list how you (and only you) can eliminate these tolerations from your life.

Tolerations What do I tolerate from others concerning my time, my money, my energy, and my love?	Changes "I" (not others) will make to eliminate this item	By when?

It is important for you to continue working on eliminating tolerations. They eat into your internal life and, if you fail to contain them, they provide too much ammunition for you to remain externally referenced. Continue to add to and work this list as new items come into your awareness.

Boundaries/Convictions Exercise

To have the space to establish your frame, you must set some limits or boundaries on your outside world. You probably were not taught this in your early life. Boundaries protect your well-being and define you as unique. Your boundaries are violated every day by people, institutions, and the screens you watch. Keeping good boundaries, therefore, is essential to being authentically who you are and staying internally referenced.

Boundary List

Check any statements that are true for you <u>most of the time</u>.

- ❑ 1. I do not allow anyone to hit me.
- ❑ 2. I do not allow anyone to yell at me.
- ❑ 3. I do not allow anyone to raise his or her voice at me.
- ❑ 4. I do not allow people to disrespect me in any way.
- ❑ 5. I do not allow anyone to shame me or make me feel guilty.
- ❑ 6. I am not involved in any activity I have felt persuaded to be in even though I did not want to be.
- ❑ 7. It is easy for me to say "no" to anyone.
- ❑ 8. I do not allow anyone to require more of me than I feel is healthy for me.
- ❑ 9. I allow no one to talk me out of my own truth.
- ❑ 10. No one takes advantage of me.
- ❑ 11. I do not allow salespeople to influence me.
- ❑ 12. I do not focus on what other people think about me.
- ❑ 13. I give other people less energy than I save for myself.
- ❑ 14. I do not allow the evening news report to bring me down.
- ❑ 15. I do not feel guilty or selfish when I do something for me.

If you left questions unchecked, your boundaries need shoring up to protect your newly emerging Authentic Self. Do not leave your Authentic Self vulnerable to the outside world. The outside world breaks through your boundaries every day by making certain demands on your time, your money, and your energy. These demands—these things you are tolerating—may be crossing your boundaries and thus controlling your personal life.

The development of emotional boundaries and the fulfillment of your needs go hand in hand. To help you, the following list gives you some ideas on how to get your needs met by setting better boundaries:

1. Identify all the ways you are different from the people around you.

2. Notice every time your opinion differs from those of other people.

3. State to someone how you disagree with him/her.

4. Disagree with a friend.

5. Spend one day taking more time being conscious of your physical needs and attending to them (example: being tired, thirsty, hungry, needing affection, etc.).

6. Notice when you need to be alone, and take the time.

Write down three boundaries you know you need to set today.

1.	
2.	
3.	

Values Exercise

Read through the list of values below and mark those that speak to you in one or more of the four corners to which they best apply to you. Add your own at the bottom if you wish.

	Physical	Mental	Emotional	Spiritual
Achievement and success	_____	_____	_____	_____
Active/not passive	_____	_____	_____	_____
Adventure and life experience	_____	_____	_____	_____
Boundaries and convictions	_____	_____	_____	_____
Independence, autonomy, and freedom	_____	_____	_____	_____
Compassion and caring	_____	_____	_____	_____
Competence	_____	_____	_____	_____
Competition and challenge	_____	_____	_____	_____
Direct communication	_____	_____	_____	_____
Emotional strength and self-awareness	_____	_____	_____	_____
Honesty and integrity	_____	_____	_____	_____
Loyalty	_____	_____	_____	_____
Intellectual/mental strength and know-how	_____	_____	_____	_____
Physical strength and health	_____	_____	_____	_____
Relationships	_____	_____	_____	_____
Resilience and optimism	_____	_____	_____	_____
Respect for self and others	_____	_____	_____	_____
Risk-taking and courage	_____	_____	_____	_____
Self-care	_____	_____	_____	_____
Selflessness and generosity	_____	_____	_____	_____
Spiritual strength and personal growth	_____	_____	_____	_____
Wisdom and insight	_____	_____	_____	_____

_____   _____ _____ _____ _____

_____   _____ _____ _____ _____

_____   _____ _____ _____ _____

Your Values Foundation

Using your list above, ask and answer the following questions about each one:

1. What are my top physical values?

    Value #1: _____

    Value #2: _____

    Value #3: _____

2. What are my most important intellectual/mental values?

    Value #1: _____

    Value #2: _____

    Value #3: _____

3. What are my important emotional values?

    Value #1: _____

    Value #2: _____

    Value #3: _____

4. What are my spiritual values?

    Value #1: _____

    Value #2: _____

    Value #3: _____

Your Code of Values: (List your top four)

#1_____

#2_____

#3_____

#4_____

FRAME

Framing Effect

Framing effect is a naturally held bias where people view decision options differently based on whether the options are presented or framed; for example, as a loss or as a gain, or as positive or negative.

When applied to an individual, the concept of frame helps us to understand how people view and treat themselves in their relationships with others, especially their closest relationships. It has helped me understand myself, my family, my clients, and how we interact.

What Is Frame?

Our frame is how we hold ourselves in the world. Frame is made up of all the conscious and unconscious beliefs we hold about ourselves, others, and the world we live in. Frame gives meaning to our words and power to our actions when we are interacting with and relating to others. Our frame gives us strength in our relationships.

Elements of Masculine Frame

Frame is a way to build internal strength and value. Establishing your frame is a personal growth and self-improvement methodology, and it's a way to live a strong, authentic life.

The masculine frame I describe has four corners: Physical, Mental/Intellectual, Emotional, and Spiritual. Establishing and maintaining frame supports a man's mission in life and his path through life. The concept of frame should be used to establish and maintain boundaries and values, manage energy/effort and time, or both. In any case, frame is a useful tool to maintain one's awareness of self and how we relate to others, especially those in our closest relationships. More significantly, we can better understand how others relate to us and when our boundaries or values are being threatened or violated.

Your Mission in Life

Your frame supports your main goal or mission in life—your life purpose. Your highest priority is always your purpose; it is <u>never</u> your spouse, wife, partner, girlfriend, boyfriend, etc. It doesn't really matter what your life purpose is, but it is always your highest priority and main focus.

Second Step – Write your masculine frame.

The first order of business was to complete the exercises in this book. Once you have established your boundaries, identified your needs and values, and eliminated tolerations, you are then ready to set up each of the four corners of your frame. Note that some boundaries and values may have an impact on more than one corner of your frame. Also, this is a living thing, just as we are. Things can change, and we can change. Your frame can change at any time you deem appropriate. However, be careful here. Be sure the changes you make do not violate boundaries or values you hold dear.

I have provided examples from my own life and work at the end of each section.

Physical Frame

Your physical frame is more than being safe, sheltered, and in good health. Your physical frame is about self-care, and it is closely connected to mental frame. Far from being healthy and free of disease, your physical frame includes lifestyle behavior choices to ensure health and avoid preventable conditions, which in turn allows you to live a dynamically balanced life that facilitates your ability to establish and maintain your mental, emotional, and spiritual frame.

Your Physical Frame:

_____

_____

_____

_____

_____

_____

_____

_____

_____

My Physical Frame:

No one may hit me. I will not tolerate physical violence upon myself or anyone else. I will maintain my physical fitness, exercise, and self-care plan. I will maintain my weight goals. I will eat properly. I will groom myself and dress neatly in current styles/fashion. I will rest properly when the need arises. I will not drink alcohol. I will not consume or smoke tobacco or illegal drugs. I will take my medications as prescribed. I will make preventative visits to my doctor periodically. I will keep my physical environment pleasing, removing tolerations as needed.

My key value: Physical strength and wellness

Mental Frame

Our mental frame is the source of our internal strength and value. Our mental frame is about how we hold ourselves in relationship to others and how we handle life's challenges. The mental frame is about being internally referenced and not influenced by the wants, needs, and desires of others. In this simple definition of mental frame lies a deeper meaning and further implications for our lives. It includes how a person thinks, their self-awareness, how they resolve their emotions (especially anger), and how they act. This is the most important component of who we are. Are your thoughts, words, and actions in alignment?

Your Mental Frame:

_____

_____

_____

_____

_____

_____

_____

_____

My Mental Frame:

No one may put me down. No one may yell or raise their voice to me. I will refrain from raising my voice to others. I will not tolerate mental abuse upon myself or others. I will do my writing every day. I will continue to learn and grow mentally. I will maintain current knowledge, abilities, and know-how to get what I want directly without manipulation. I will not let myself be manipulated by others, maintaining my awareness about how I think, feel, and react in all situations. I will continue my research. I will continue to take guitar lessons to maintain mental/physical integration capability. I will take time to unplug (no blue screens) in the evenings before retiring. I will take downtime as needed during the day. I will take action to maintain my mental sharpness as I deem fit. I will remove mental tolerations as they arise.

My key value: Mental health and energy

Emotional Frame

Emotions tell us our truth. There are no bad emotions, but some emotions are uncomfortable.

Your emotional frame is not the absence of emotions; it is your ability to be aware of and to understand your emotions, and what they are telling you. In your emotions lies the truth of things for you. If you can figure out what is going on with you emotionally, you can understand the truth of things for yourself. It is important that you do not allow yourself to be controlled by your emotions but use them to move your life forward in positive directions.

Your Emotional Frame:

_____

_____

_____

_____

_____

_____

My Emotional Frame:

No one may make me feel "less than." I will not tolerate emotional violence (see note below) upon myself or others. I will maintain my emotional self-awareness by doing my morning writing/ journaling every day. I will control my own emotions, but not allow myself to be controlled by my emotions. I will not react to any situations in an emotionally charged manner, rather choosing to respond appropriately without emotion. Emotional self-awareness, what I am feeling, and the meaning of those emotions is key to insight and a litmus test as to what is true for me in any given situation. How I feel about something determines what is true for me about it. I will always attempt to understand others' emotions but not allow myself to be influenced by them; they are their responsibility. I will express my emotions as and when I become aware of them. I will express my truth as and when I become aware of it.

Note: Emotional violence is defined as the process by which one person diminishes or destroys the inner life of another.

My key value: Emotional self-awareness, high emotional set-point, and neutral response

Spiritual Frame

Your soul, your spiritual frame is the core resource for building strong internal value and is the key component of one's journey of recovery and healing. This is the healing that takes place in recovery treatment centers, residential programs, and trauma recovery. I believe our highest purpose is to grow our inner life ourselves. My effort is placed on working on myself, my inner life.

Your Spiritual Frame:

_____

_____

_____

_____

_____

_____

_____

_____

_____

_____

_____

My Spiritual Frame:

I will continue spiritual growth and the development of my authentic self (true self) as my highest priority. I will not allow my daily spiritual practice to be violated in any way. I will maintain my spiritual awareness through my daily writing as it relates to my emotions and my connection to the deepest part of my soul/spirit. I will meditate twice a day. I will continue to integrate positive change into my life when and wherever possible. I will always attempt to live in the moment, seeking to not focus or think about the past or future as much as possible.

My key value: Spiritual connection with my soul

Summarize Your Frame

_____

_____

_____

_____

_____

_____

_____

_____

_____

_____

_____

_____

_____

_____

_____

_____

_____

_____

_____

_____

_____

_____

_____

_____

The Truth

This is the truth of who you are.

Your physical frame provides clarity on your physical boundaries. It defines what you will and, more importantly, will not tolerate. It includes lifestyle and behavior choices relating to not doing things that are bad for you and doing things that are good for you to ensure health and avoid preventable diseases. It will allow you to live a healthy life that supports your ability to establish and maintain your mental, emotional, and spiritual frame.

Your mental frame provides clarity on your boundaries and how you see yourself in the world. It should include your mental models, your limiting and empowering beliefs about what is true for you. This determines your internal strength and value. It includes how you think, how you handle your emotions (especially anger and sadness), and how you act. Done thoroughly, this will provide the basis for becoming internally referenced (vs. externally referenced), thus minimizing the influence of outside factors on your behavior. You will no longer be concerned about what other people think of you; it is none of your business.

Your emotional frame is primarily related to listening to yourself and being aware of which emotions you are experiencing and what they are telling you, without being triggered by them. It is not the absence of emotions nor is it the suppressing of emotions; it is your ability to be aware of and to understand your emotions and what they are telling you. This self-awareness is critically important to your emotional health.

Your spiritual frame defines the boundaries of your own sacred "inner life," which I emphasize as so important to happiness. From this, you derive the inner strength to prevail over adversity and hardship, as well as cope with life's day-to-day challenges. How we nurture our inner relationship with ourselves is a lifelong endeavor.

Testing Frame

You now have the basis to determine when your frame is being tested. Your frame will be tested. When your boundaries, convictions, or values are being bent or broken by someone, you are being tested. Are you aware of what you will tolerate and what you will not tolerate? Are you aware of your Code of Values and your boundaries—your frame? Are you communicating your frame to others? If you are, then you are ready to face any test that comes your way.

Every time your frame is tested, you must push back. If you don't stand up and push back, things will only get worse. You must always say something, but you must say it without emotion. You must remain cool and emotionally non-reactive, solid in every dimension.

With your significant other, you must stand firm against her storms, an oak tree. When she is in the middle of an emotional storm, it is you who must be there—strong, solid, unshakable, and immovable—to protect her and defend her until her storm passes. Protect her, and you protect the relationship. Stand up to her, and you stand up for the relationship. You must be her shelter from her own storms. You must remain internally referenced and not allow yourself to be diverted off your path nor into external reference in any circumstance.

When I was at my pleasing, suck-up, nice-guy worst, I was clearly in the external reference mode. Pleasing others, or doing what I thought others expected of me, is nice guy, pleasing behavior. This behavior is clearly repulsive and a big turn-off to anyone in my life. That person no longer exists.

A True Man

After doing this work, I felt remarkably stronger in every respect.

- I have a strong masculine frame, boundaries, and values, which are resilient under testing.

- I am living my life with purpose. My purpose, mission, and path through life are my highest priority.

- I am a man of action, not at all passive.

- I am internally motivated, focused, and referenced. I am influenced very little by others or outside factors.

- I am self-responsible. I am not a victim. I am responsible for everything that shows up in my life.

- I am focused on self-improvement—always self-transforming. I realize I cannot change other people, so I must change myself. And that change is a never-ending process.

- I am self-aware. I know my truth and can speak my truth. I always have an opinion and speak my opinion directly. I ask for what I want and need directly, without manipulation.

- I am living in integrity—thoughts, feelings, words, and actions are in alignment. This results in my internal attunement. I do what I say. I do the right thing even when no one is watching.

- I maintain a high emotional set point and high energy. I have a powerful presence. I fear nothing.

I am, however, not finished. As I have said before, personal growth is always a work in progress and is never complete. I will always be open to new ways to learn and grow. It is a life-long process.

"Tell the truth. Or, at least, don't lie."

—Jordan B. Peterson, PhD

References

Lewis, Michael M. <u>The Undoing Project</u>. New York: W.W. Norton & Co. 2017.

Kahneman, D., & Tversky, A. (1984). "Choices, values, and frames." *American Psychologist, 39*(4), 341–350.

Snow, D. A.; Rochford, E. B.; Worden, S. K.; Benford, R. D. (1986). "Frame alignment processes, micro-mobilization, and movement participation". *American Sociological Review*. **51**(4): 464–481.

Tversky, Amos, and Kahneman, Daniel (1981). "The Framing of Decisions and the Psychology of Choice". *Science*. **211**(4481): 453–58.

Tversky, Amos, and Daniel Kahneman. "Rational Choice and the Framing of Decisions." *The Journal of Business*, vol. 59, no. 4, University of Chicago Press, 1986, pp. S251–78.

CPSIA information can be obtained
at www.ICGtesting.com
Printed in the USA
BVHW090233010222
627651BV00013B/775